39092062228103
10/10/2006
Campbell, Jean,
Getting started stringing
beads /

P9-DWK-044

Albany County Public Library
Laramie, WY
*Where your books came from in
2005-2006:*

Book
Donations
23%

Cash
Donations
14%

Taxes
63%

GETTING STARTED

stringing
beads

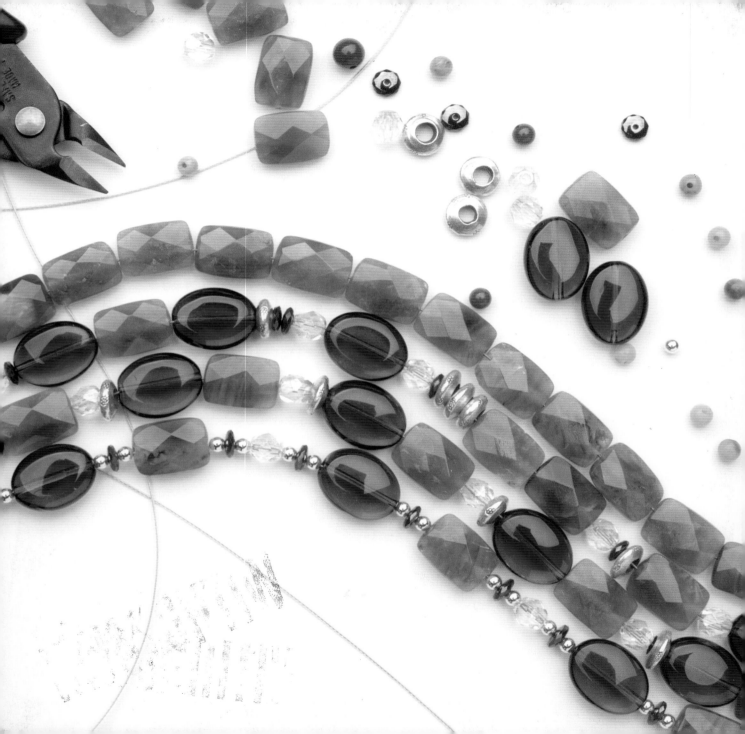

GETTING STARTED

stringing
beads

Jean **Campbell**

 **Interweave Press**

Albany County
Public Library
Laramie, Wyoming

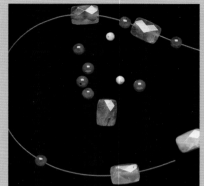

Project editor: Christine Townsend
Technical editor: Bonnie Brooks
Photography: Joe Coca and Jean Campbell
Photo styling: Paulette Livers
Cover and interior design: Paulette Livers
Illustrations: Ann Swanson
Production: Samantha L. Thaler
Copy editor: Stephen Beal
Proofreader and indexer: Nancy Arndt

Text copyright © 2005 Interweave Press
Photography copyright © 2005 Joe Coca and Interweave Press, Inc.

All rights reserved.

 INTERWEAVE PRESS

201 East Fourth Street
Loveland, CO 80537-5655 USA
www.interweave.com

Printed in China by C & C Offset Printing Co., Ltd.

Library of Congress Cataloging-in-Publication Data
Getting started stringing beads / Jean Campbell, editor.
      p. cm.
  Includes index.
  ISBN 1-931499-79-9
  1. Beadwork. 2. Jewelry making. I. Campbell, Jean, 1964-
  TT860.G48 2005
  745.58'2--dc22

10 9 8 7 6 5 4 3 2 1

acknowledgments

A big thanks to the Interweave book family—Betsy Armstrong, Nancy Arndt, Stephen Beal, Bonnie Brooks, Laura Levaas, Linda Ligon, Paulette Livers, Linda Stark, Ann Swanson, Samantha Thaler, and Christine Townsend—for taking this book from an idea discussed at a Tucson stoplight to a beautiful thing you can hold in your hands.

To my friends at The Bead Monkey for letting me loose with a camera in their shop. And to employee Anna Tollin for helping me in a pinch.

To the very supportive *Beadwork* magazine staff: Jamie Hogsett and Dustin Wedekind for sharing their wealth of bead know-how and Danielle Fox for her eagle eye.

To my husband Joe Campbell for his unwavering confidence and for always making me laugh, especially when I'm up to here in beads.

To my son Dylan, for his insightful gift of pointing out the obvious, and to my daughter Emma, for her welcome interruptions of smiles and laughter. They are both rays of sunshine, even when I serve macaroni and cheese every night for weeks at a time.

And to the contributors and readers of *Beadwork* magazine who have taught me just about everything I know about beads.

contents

introduction

Maybe a friend made a necklace and told you it was easy. Then you saw a bracelet in a shop window and wondered if you could make one just like it—or even better. The next step had you walking past a bead shop and your inspiration soared at the sight of all the fabulous beads! However it happened, you've had your first introduction to the world of beading and you're hungry to learn more.

Learning to string beads is a great first step in jewelry-making. It's easy, quick, saves money on accessories, and gives you the opportunity to have wonderful new things in your jewelry box. But most importantly, stringing your own necklaces, earrings, and bracelets gives you creative satisfaction. And there's an added benefit: the process of stringing bead after bead is engagingly meditative.

In this book you'll learn the basics of bead stringing—how to connect, crimp, and create and I'm sure its continued guidance will make you confident about stringing beads. I've included chapters on shopping for beads, the stringing basics, and working with strung bead patterns and focal beads. I've added a little wireworking instruction to make you completely efficient. And you'll find a chapter on designing your own pieces to top it all off. Armed with all this knowledge, you'll be designing your own beautiful jewelry in no time.

The book's clear illustrations and photographs will benefit your learning. I suggest you move chapter by chapter, using the "lessons" as a sort of Beading 101. If you do, the next time you visit a bead shop you'll move with confidence from bead tray to bead tray, and once you get home you'll know just what to do with your purchases.

So get ready to string! And have a great time.

If you're a beginner just venturing out into the world of beading, you'll need this book as your guide.

The Bead Shopping Experience

GETTING STARTED

Walking into a bead shop for the first time can be intimidating! All those beads hanging on the walls, displayed on tables, and hiding underneath counters are just plain scary. But underneath the apparent jumble, there really is organization and purpose.

This section of our Beading 101 describes the shopping experience. I'm sure you have lots of questions …

SHOPPING TRAYS

Most shops have trays, baskets, or bowls by the door or at the counter for you to put your selections in—think of them as mini shopping carts. And, most times, you'll find a slip of paper, plastic bags, or check slips with a pen inside these trays for you to write down the price of your individual bead selections. For example, if you choose two beads and they are $1 each, then you'd write 2 @ $1. In most shops, writing the price down on the slip is only for loose beads, not for those items that are already marked.

Strands of beads are strung on inexpensive thread. Do not use this thread in your jewelry projects, as it is not sturdy enough for wearables.

THE SHOP

Walk around the entire shop first before you make any selections. This way you'll have a sense of what you'd like to take home. You'll see that the shop organizes its wares by type of bead. Loose beads are on tables or in trays; tubes of Japanese seed beads are usually placed in bins; hanks hang on the wall. Strands of semi-precious stone, pearl, and bone often hang on the wall as well, and expensive items, such as crystals, sterling silver, and findings are often kept behind the shop's counter. Basically, beads are found with like beads.

SHOP EMPLOYEES

Don't be afraid to ask the people who work at the shop for help—that's what they're there for! They really are the experts since they answer both beginners' and advanced beaders' inquiries all day long. They're usually eager to help you with the simplest questions, and if you can't find something you're looking for, they probably know exactly where it is.

BEAD TYPES

A bead can be made of just about anything, but here are some of the usual goodies you'll find at your local shop.

Bone and horn beads are inexpensive handmade beads that usually come from Indonesia and the Philippines; they're created from the bone or horns of working animals such as goats, camels, and cattle. Initially white, bone beads can be dyed any color.

Bugle beads are glass beads made of varying lengths of cut glass cane. These long, thin beads are sized by number—1, 2, 3, and 5. Use durable thread, beading wire, or a seed bead between bugle beads, as their sharp edges can cut your thread or wire.

Cloisonné (pronounced *kloy-zen-A*) *beads* are made of enamel fired on a background of brass to produce a stained-glass effect.

Crystal beads most often come from Austria. Crisp facets and a clean finish on these leaded glass beads make them sparkle. Request crystal beads by size (in millimeter) and shape (round, bicone, drop, and cube). Use a durable beading wire with crystal beads because their sharp edges can cause the wire to wear.

Fire-polished beads are Czech glass beads that start as rounds and are then hand- or machine-faceted to catch the light. A surface finish is often added to create extra sparkle. Request fire-polished beads by size (in millimeter).

Horn beads (see Bone beads).

India glass beads are rough wound beads made in India by machines that wrap molten glass around mandrels.

Lampworked beads are artistic handmade beads created with hot glass spun onto a mandrel over a flame. Since some lampworked beads can be exceptionally heavy, use stringing materials appropriate for the weight of your bead.

Metal beads vary in type of metal, shape, and size, but they're a wonderful complement to glass and stone beads.

- ***Base metal beads,*** the least expensive option, are comprised of nonprecious metals such as aluminum, brass, bronze, copper, and nickel.

- ***Gold-filled beads*** are those in which 1/10 of 12k gold is applied to the surface of brass or another base metal. The resulting bead is very strong.

- ***Silver and 18k gold plated beads*** are created by an electroplating process. A very thin layer of silver or gold is applied to another type of metal like brass or copper.

- ***Sterling silver beads*** are a mix of silver and copper. To be sold legally as sterling the percentages must be 92.5 percent pure silver and 7.5 percent copper. Sterling silver is prone to tarnishing (see tips for cleaning it on page 86). While some people have allergic skin reactions when wearing less pure metal jewelry, most can wear sterling silver jewelry without such reactions.

- ***Vermeil*** (pronounced vehr-MAY) ***beads*** are made of sterling silver electroplated with gold.

Freshwater pearl beads are often just called "pearls" at bead shops. These pearls are less expensive than the pearls in your mother's jewelry box. They come in all sizes and shapes and are made by clams or mussels in China, Japan, and the United States. When you're buying pearls, be careful to note where the drill hole is, as many have off-center holes. Use a very thin beading wire or thread and needle to string these beads.

Polymer clay beads are colorful handmade plasticine (a clay-like substance made of synthetic materials) beads that are fired at low temperatures. They are relatively light when strung.

Pony beads are made with glass, wood, or plastic and are shaped like seed beads but are larger (sizes 6°–8°). Crow beads are even larger, coming in sizes from 6mm–9mm.

Pressed-glass beads are colorful pressed-glass beads from Czechoslovakia. The beads are also called Czech glass, and come in shapes ranging from simple rounds, ovals, and squares to leaves and flowers.

Resin beads are translucent and very durable beads available in bright, candylike colors.

Seed beads are tiny pieces of a thin, long glass cane that are melted slightly or tumbled to round the edges.

- *Cylinder beads* (brand names: Aikos, Delicas, Magnificas, and Treasures), are another type of seed bead; they are perfectly cylindrical beads with thin walls and large holes. They come in two sizes—regular and large, which approximate a size 11° seed bead and a size 8° seed bead. The degree mark next to the size stands for "aught." It is a traditional beading term/symbol; its origin is obscure, but its archaic meaning points to "or so" or "zero."

- *Czech seed beads* come on hanks, are shaped like tiny donuts, and are slightly irregular. They are sized from 20° to 6°. "Charlottes" are Czech seed beads with facets that make them sparkle.

- *Japanese seed beads* are sold in tubes or by the kilo and are shaped like rounded cylinders. They come in 6°, 8°, 11°, and 14/15° sizes.

A hank is a gathering of twelve strands of seed beads. The price of a hank is for the whole gathering, not for a single strand.

SEED BEAD SIZES

7
8
9
10
11
12
14

Bead Size	Beads Per Inch	Beads per Gram	Wt. in Grams of 12-strand hank
16°	28	275-325	22.5
14°	25	250-300	22
13°	24	150-200	33
12°	21	125-175	33.5
11°	18	100-150	34.5
10°	16	75-125	38.5
9°	12	50-100	38.5

Japanese seed beads are usually sold loose in tubes or bags.

Semiprecious stone beads range from amethyst to zebra jasper—A to Z! They come in all sizes and shapes, but generally they are polished and faceted, donut-shaped, rough-cut, or chips. These beads are usually heavy, so use a strong beading wire to string them.

Shell beads are created from natural shells. The iridescent substance that is formed in mollusk shells is marketed as mother-of-pearl.

Wood beads are generally inexpensive beads made from Asian indigenous woods. Many are handmade. All are lightweight and a nice addition to ethnic-looking pieces.

MILLIMETER SIZE CHART

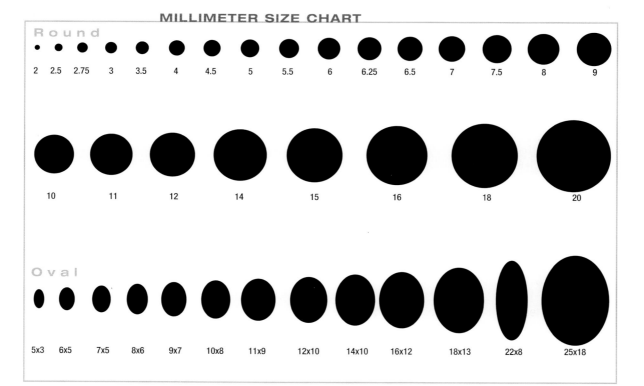

Round

| 2 | 2.5 | 2.75 | 3 | 3.5 | 4 | 4.5 | 5 | 5.5 | 6 | 6.25 | 6.5 | 7 | 7.5 | 8 | 9 |

| 10 | 11 | 12 | 14 | 15 | 16 | 18 | 20 |

Oval

| 5x3 | 6x5 | 7x5 | 8x6 | 9x7 | 10x8 | 11x9 | 12x10 | 14x10 | 16x12 | 18x13 | 22x8 | 25x18 |

In most bead stores, you'll find everything organized and labeled for easy shopping.

BEAD SHAPES CHART

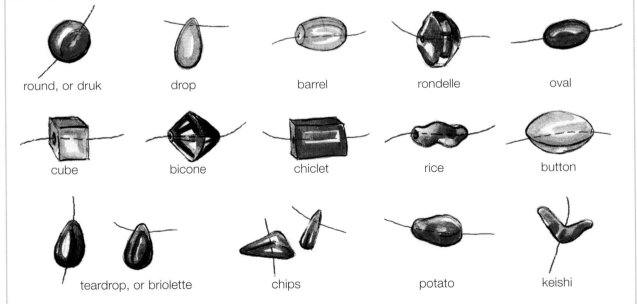

round, or druk

drop

barrel

rondelle

oval

cube

bicone

chiclet

rice

button

teardrop, or briolette

chips

potato

keishi

STRINGING MATERIALS

Nothing is worse than having your jewelry stretch, snag, or fall apart when you've worked so hard to put it together, so for each piece you make, consider that the stringing materials are as important, if not more so, than the beads! It is the threads, cord, or wire that keep your beads together and allows them to be wearable and beautiful for a long time. Here are several stringing materials and suggestions on how to use them.

Beading wire (brand names Accuflex, Acculon, Beadalon, Soft Flex) is a very flexible nylon-coated multistrand steel wire available in diameters from .010 to .024. Choose the widest diameter for large, heavy, or abrasive beads; a medium diameter for crystals and small lampworked beads; and the smallest diameter for beads with small holes like pearls and seed beads. Use a wire cutter to cut this stringing material.

Braided thread (brand names Dandy Line and PowerPro) is an extremely strong, synthetic thread also used for fishing. It has great strength (10–20 pound test), is very thin (.006 diameter), can be knotted, and comes in two colors—moss green and white. Because of the angle of their blades, children's Fiskars scissors cut these materials better than other scissors.

Elastic cord (monofilament, Illusion cord) comes in wide (1 mm) and thin (.5 mm) styles and is best used for stretch bracelets. Secure this cord with knots or crimp tubes. Use a scissors to cut it.

Hemp cord is made up of natural fibers and is the best selection for macramé. Use a scissors to cut this cord. This cord can be cut with a scissors.

Leather cord is a round, smooth cord that comes in a variety of colors, can be knotted, and is best used for wide-holed, large beads. This cord can be cut with a scissors.

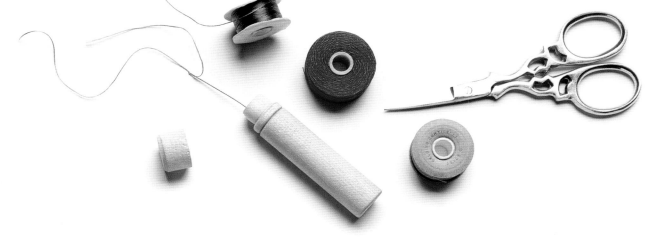

Memory wire is extremely hard, coiled wire that does not lose its shape. It comes in different sizes for necklaces, bracelets, and rings. Cut this wire with a memory wire cutters or by bending it back and forth. Do not use a regular wire cutter or the wire will mar the jaws.

Nylon thread (brand names C-Lon, Nymo, and Silamide) is thin synthetic thread that you purchase by the spool like regular sewing thread. Nylon is best used for lightweight stringing projects that require a needle and thread. This cord can be cut with a scissors.

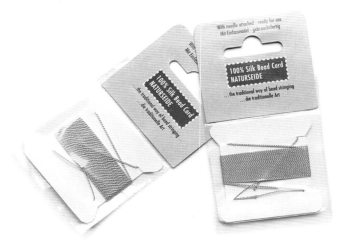

Silk thread and cord come in a variety of colors and widths. They are sold by the spool or on a card (often with a built-in needle). The thin thread is the best choice for stringing pearls, and the wider cord works well for knotting techniques. Prestretch this material (pull the ends apart several times) before you use it. This material can be cut with a scissors.

Suede cord is a rough strip of Ultrasuede that works well for wide-holed beads. You can cut it with scissors.

Sterling silver wire is the best choice for wirework (for our simple stringing purposes, wirework means creating wire loops for things like dangles or earrings). It is relatively soft so it's easily manipulated, but has good memory. Cut this material with wire cutters.

Stringing materials in the shop.

TOOLS

You'll need tools to put your masterpiece together. There's a plethora of tools for beading, but here are the ones to get your bead box stashed for stringing.

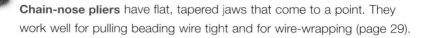

Chain-nose pliers have flat, tapered jaws that come to a point. They work well for pulling beading wire tight and for wire-wrapping (page 29).

Crimping pliers squeeze and secure a crimp tube onto beading wire. (See instructions about how to crimp on page 20.)

Flat-nose pliers have flat, tapered jaws. Use them for pulling beading wire tight and to wire-wrap (page 29).

Round-nose pliers have round, tapered jaws that come to a point. Use these pliers to make simple loops and to do wire-wrapping (page 28).

Split-ring pliers have a flat, pointed, tapered jaw on one side, and on the other side a bent tip for opening split rings.

Wire cutters have sharp jaws with which to cut beading wire, head pins, eye pins, and other soft wire.

Crimping pliers

Round-nose pliers

Chain-nose pliers

Wire cutters

Flat-nose pliers

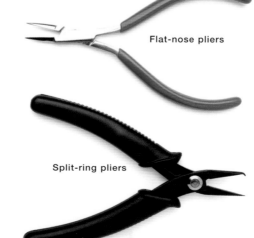

Split-ring pliers

BEADING NEEDLES

Beading needles are very fine, long (up to 3"/7.6 cm) needles whose eyes are the same width as the rest of the needle—an important feature when you consider the added width of the stringing material. Beading needles work well for very small-holed beads like small seed beads, pearls, and some semiprecious stones. Because the eye size is so small, beading needles can be a challenge to thread. To make it easier, place the stringing material between the thumb and forefinger of your nondominant hand, allowing just a small amount of the end to peek out. Use your dominant hand to place the needle eye on the end and pull it through.

Big-eye needles come in 2¼" and 5" (5.7 and 12.7 cm) lengths and have pointed ends with a double wire down the center. They are the easiest needles to thread—simply separate the center wires, place the stringing material between, and allow the wires to collapse on themselves to capture the thread. These needles work well for fairly small-holed beads, and the 5"– (12.7-cm) long version is especially useful in stringing because you can easily see if you've strung your beads in the correct order.

Twisted wire needles are made of fine wire and feature a large loop on one end and a twisted shank on the other. You thread the stringing material through the loop and, as you pass the needle through a bead, the loop collapses to secure the stringing material. Twisted-wire needles are generally one-use and work well for small-holed beads such as pearls.

If you are stringing beads with very small holes, you may need to use a needle to pass the stringing material through. Here are the most common and useful needles to get the job done.

The Basics from Start to Finish

Stringing is the first beading technique you learn. Remember the yarn and macaroni necklaces you made in kindergarten? Stringing with beads is the same thing, but this time you're making real jewelry with professional materials. Stringing is a great way to start off in the world of beads. But even for stringing you need to know the basics. Here are a few to get you on your way.

STRINGING BEADS

Use stringing material (needle and thread, beading wire, elastic, leather) to pass through the holes of beads.

Tip Don't pick up beads and place them on the end of the stringing material; instead, scoop up the beads on the needle or thread end from a nonroll surface such as a blanket, dishcloth, or piece of suede.

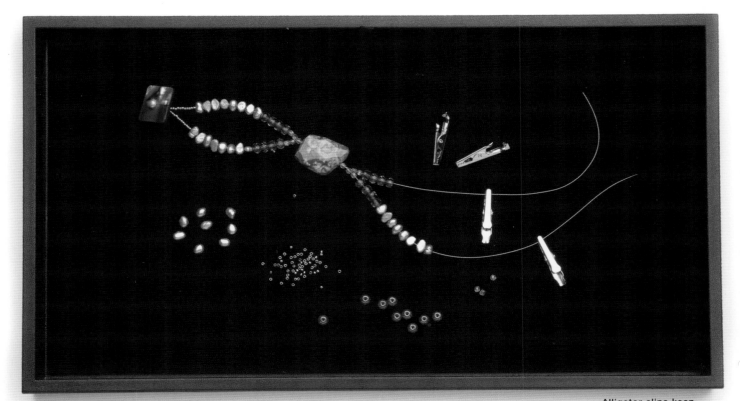

Alligator clips keep beads from falling off beading wire.

Tip

If a project says to string beads before you secure a clasp, use a tension bead to keep the beads from slipping off the other end of the stringing material. Make a tension bead by stringing a bead and passing through it again. When you are ready to secure the end of the thread, simply remove the tension bead.

A tension bead doesn't work very well if you are using beading wire. Instead, use transparent tape or alligator clips to secure the end.

Tension bead

CRIMPING

Use crimp tubes to secure the end of a beading wire to a clasp or connector. Be patient—this technique takes a little practice, but it ensures a tight closure and professional look every time.

Step 1: Begin your strand of beads with a crimp tube.

Step 2: Pass through the clasp or connector.

Step 3: Pass back through the crimp tube and, if possible, a few beads on the strand.

Step 4: Snug the crimp tube and beads close to the closure.

Step 5: Spread the two wires so they line each side of the tube. Use the first notch on the crimping pliers (round on one jaw, dipped on the other) to squeeze the crimp tube shut, making sure there's one wire on each side of the crimp.

Step 6: Use the second notch on the crimping pliers (rounded on both jaws) to shape the tube into a tight round. Make gentle squeezes around the tube for a perfect cylinder.

Step 7: Trim the tail wire close to the beads.

General instructions are given here to show how to make the clasp, but you may need to modify the number of seed beads to tailor the clasp to your specific button or large bead.

Step 1: Use a shank button to make an anchor for the clasp. To start, measure enough beading wire to complete a one-stranded necklace or bracelet. String 1 crimp tube and the button. Pass back through the crimp tube. If the shank is wide enough, string enough seed beads to pass through the shank and back into the crimp tube. Snug the beads and crimp the tube.

You can also use a bead (9mm or larger) to act as the anchor for your clasp. To begin this technique, measure enough beading wire to complete a one-stranded necklace or bracelet. String 1 crimp tube, the large bead, and 1–3 seed beads. Pass back through the large bead and the crimp tube. Snug the beads and crimp the tube.

Step 2: String enough seed beads so that as you lay the strand across the back of the shank button, the end reaches the edge of the button. If you are using a large bead as the anchor, string 1–5 seed beads.

Step 3: String the beads for the body of the necklace or bracelet.

Step 4: String 3 seed beads and 1 crimp tube. String enough seed beads so that when you pass back through the crimp tube the loop slides snugly over the button or large bead. Remove or add seed beads as necessary, pass back through the crimp tube, snug all the beads, and crimp.

MAKING SEED BEAD LOOPS

This homemade toggle clasp is an alternative to its metal counterparts. The design is particularly effective when you wish to work a special button or large bead into the final design, and it often gives the overall piece more unity, especially if you use colors and bead types that you are going to use in the necklace or bracelet.

KNOTTING

The knots you use in stringing beads sometimes secure materials, other times make them more beautiful, and often accomplish both! Here are several among which to choose.

Double connection knot (or X knot)

Double Connection (or X) knots allow a bead or pendant to butt up squarely against the knot, and is most often used with thicker leather or silk cord.

Step 1: Pass the right cord under the left cord, over the top of both cords, and under and through the loop between them.

Step 2: Pass the left cord over and under the right cord, through the left outside loop created in Step 1, over the left cord, and through the loop you just created. Adjust the knot and pull tight.

Figure 8 knots are secure knots that don't kink the thread, cord, or beading wire.

Step 1: Lay one end of the stringing material over the other end to make a loop.

Step 2: Pass the top cord (the working cord) over and behind the bottom one.

Step 3: Pass the working cord over itself and through the loop created in Step 2. Pull tight.

Figure 8 knot

Lark's head knots are great for securing the stringing material to a cord or bar.

Step 1: Fold the stringing material in half.

Step 2: Bend the fold over the bar.

Step 3: Pull the ends through the loop created in Step 2 and tighten.

Lark's head knot

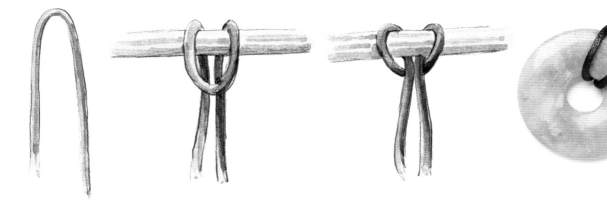

Overhand knot

The overhand knot is the basic knot for tying off thread. It is not very secure, so use it sparingly.

Step 1: Make a loop with the stringing material.

Step 2: Pass the cord that lies behind the loop over the front cord and through the loop. Pull tight.

Surgeon's knot

Surgeon's knots are very secure knots for finishing off stringing materials.

Step 1: Tie an overhand knot, right over left, but instead of one twist over the left cord, make at least two.

Step 2: Tie an overhand knot, left over right, and pull tight.

Slide knots are great for finishing off leather-strung jewelry. Because they move up and down the cord, slide knots offer a wide range of style possibilities.

Step 1: Place the left cord next to the right cord in opposite directions.

Step 2: Bend the right cord end back about 3" (7.5 cm). Coil it around itself and the left cord until you make three coils.

Step 3: Weave the right cord end through the coil and pull tight. Trim the tail end close to the knot.

Square knots are the classic sturdy knots suitable for most stringing materials.

Step 1: Make an overhand knot, passing the right end over the left end.

Step 2: Make another overhand knot, this time passing the left end over the right end. Pull tight.

ADDING KNOT CUPS

When stringing beads with thread it's best to use a knot cup to create a connector to the clasp or other closure. The knot cup adds strength and creates a secure connection. Using a seed bead between the knot cup and the knot secures the thread even more. Here is how to add the cups.

Step 1: Tie a strong knot at the end of the thread.

Step 2: String a seed bead and pass through the inside of the knot cup.

Step 3: Close the knot cup so the seed bead and knot are inside it, trim the tail thread, and bend down the looped closure. String the beads for the piece.

Step 4: String a knot cup from the outside in and a seed bead.

Step 5: Snug all the beads tightly and tie a strong knot to secure all. Close the knot cup so the seed bead and knot are inside it, trim the thread, and bend down the looped closure.

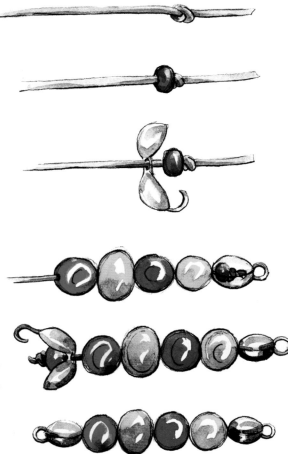

Sometimes you'll want to use knots to secure and space beads along the strung strand. Do so by adding one bead at a time and tying one knot at a time with a needle and thread. The process starts after you've tied on a knot cup (see page 26 for knot cup instructions), added French wire (see page 33), or simply knotted onto a clasp. Here are three steps to neat, clean knots.

(see page 26 ... see page 33)

KNOTTING BETWEEN BEADS

Step 1: String a bead with your needle and pull it against the knot cup. Form a loose overhand knot next to the bead.

Step 2: Put the needle through the knot and slightly within the bead hole so that it holds the thread tightly against the bead. Pull on the thread to tighten the knot, keeping the needle that holds the thread stable against the bead.

Step 3: Tighten the knot and remove the needle.

Tips

- If you are using silk thread with a needle already attached, it's easier to use a second, more sturdy needle to knot between beads.
- When measuring cord for knotting, multiply the desired length of your piece by three. This will give you plenty of length to make the knots.
- When knotting beads, take into account the space the knots take up so you can plan the total length of the piece. To figure out the extra length, tie a knot on your stringing material, string a bead, and simply measure the length. Multiply the length by the number of beads you'd like to add and you'll find your total necklace or bracelet length.

WIRE-WORKING

Many stringing projects assume you know a little something about working with wire—especially when you create earrings. Here are a few simple techniques you'll need to know for the projects in this book.

Chain is used for charm bracelets and chandelier earrings in this book. When you cut chain with wire cutters, count one extra link, then what is required for the project. The link you cut can be used as a jump ring later.

Jump rings are most often used to connect wirework to findings. When you open a jump ring, use two pliers and bend the ends laterally, not apart

(see right). Add the finding and close the jump ring with the two pliers. Be sure to close the jump ring completely so that your finding doesn't slip out. Do so by closing the ends slightly farther than where the ends match up—the wire will spring back to the right position.

Simple loops turn a piece of wire into a semisecure connector for jump rings or other findings. They are most often used to finish dangles for jewelry or to make rosary chains. Make a double loop (a very secure loop) by turning the round-nose pliers twice to make two loops side by side.

Step 1: Grasp one end of a piece of wire with a round-nose pliers.

Step 2: Hold onto the wire with one hand and gently turn the pliers until the wire end and wire stem touch.

Step 3: For a clean finish, continue to hold onto the loop with round-nose pliers as you use flat-nose pliers to make a ninety-degree reverse bend where the loop ends.

Spirals are a decorative way to finish earring or other jewelry dangles.

Step 1: Make a small loop at the end of the wire with a round-nose pliers.

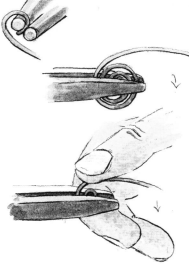

Step 2: Enlarge the loop by holding onto the small loop with a chain-nose pliers and pushing the wire around the loop with your thumb.

Step 3: Enlarge the spiral by letting go of the chain-nose pliers and repositioning the spiral within the pliers' jaws to draw the wire over the previous loops.

Wrapped loops are a very secure way to turn a piece of wire into a connector for jump rings or other findings. They're a bit difficult to master, but keep trying!

Step 1: Make a ninety-degree bend 2" from one end of the wire.

Step 2: Use round-nose pliers to hold the wire near the angle and bend the short end of the wire up and around the pliers until the wire meets itself.

Step 3: Wrap the wire tail tightly down the stem of the wire to create two or three coils. Trim the excess wire.

A STRING AND A THING

If you'd like to go easy with stringing, just find a string and a thing! Large pendants work well for this technique, but smaller beads work well, too, as long as the stringing material is thin enough to fit through the smaller hole.

Materials

Pendants

Notions

Leather, suede, sateen cord, ribbon

String the pendant or bead on a material of your choice. Keep the pendant in place by tying a knot (see page 22) on each side, or forget the knots and let it slide back and forth. Tie a knot to secure the necklace around your neck. It's easy!

ALL ABOUT FINDINGS

FINDINGS ILLUSTRATED

Chances are when you went bead shopping you ran into a bunch of little metal things called findings. They are clasps and other connectors that keep pieces together. You don't need to know what they all do at first, because the more you bead, the more you'll learn your way around findings. In the meantime, here are descriptions of some of the most common ones.

Bead caps are domed pieces that fit over the end of beads for extra decoration. String them first from the outside in, string a bead, and string the next bead cap from the inside out. The caps should fit snugly.

Bullion (also known as French wire or gimp) is a fine hollow coil of wire that you string at the connection between the beaded strand and a finding. The coil strengthens the connection and adds a professional look. To use, string ¼" (2.5 cm) or so of bullion after you've strung the last bead. String the clasp or connector, pass back through the last bead added, and secure.

Chain is links of soldered metal loops that act as a base for many jewelry projects. Connect beads and clasps to this finding with jump or split rings.

Clasps connect the ends of a necklace or bracelet. Some have one loop for single-strand jewelry, others have two or more loops for multistrand pieces. Here are seven of the most common.

Box clasps are shaped like a box on one end and have a bent metal tab on the other end that snaps into the box under its own tension. Many are decorated with beautiful designs.

Fish hook clasps are most commonly used with the classic pearl necklace and have a hook on one end that catches inside a marquis-shaped box.

Hook and eye clasps are comprised of a J-shaped side and a loop side that hook into each other. This clasp requires tension to keep it closed, so it's best used with necklaces that have some weight.

Lobster and spring ring clasps have levers that operate an internal spring to open and close them. Hook the clasp on a jump ring that's been added at the other end of the jewelry to secure. Incorporate these clasps into small, delicate pieces.

Magnetic clasps are held together by strong magnets and should only be used for light- to middle-weight pieces. Magnetic clasps should not be used by people with pacemakers.

S hooks are made up of an S-shaped wire with jump rings at each end. This clasp, like the hook and eye, depends on tension to keep it closed.

Toggle clasps require tension to keep them shut. The bar passes through the ring perpendicularly and closes when it's parallel. These clasps can be used on any piece that hangs or is tight-fitting, and they work especially well for heavier necklaces.

Earring findings are the pieces of metal that make a connection between the beadwork and the ear. There are several different styles.

Clip-ons are nonpierced ear findings that tighten the metal against the ear with a spring. Glue the beadwork to the flat portion of the clip, or attach it to the loop at the front of the clip.

French ear wires are J-shaped pierced-ear findings that have a loop on one end to connect to the beadwork. To use, open the loop as you would a jump ring, add a strung dangle, and close the loop.

Hoops are circular pierced-ear findings comprised of fine wire. Add beads by sliding them over the circle of wire, and make a gentle bend on the non-loop end to secure.

Kidney ear wires are pieced-ear findings comprised of a single piece of wire. Connect the beadwork to the dip near the locking portion.

Lever backs have a spring that opens to allow you to put the wire through your ear and then closes to secure it. Connect the beadwork by opening the loop at the bottom of the finding.

Posts are pierced-ear findings made up of a straight piece of wire with a stopper on one end; they're secured with an ear nut. Connect the beadwork to the loop below the stopper. Do so by opening the loop like a jump ring, adding the dangle, and closing the loop.

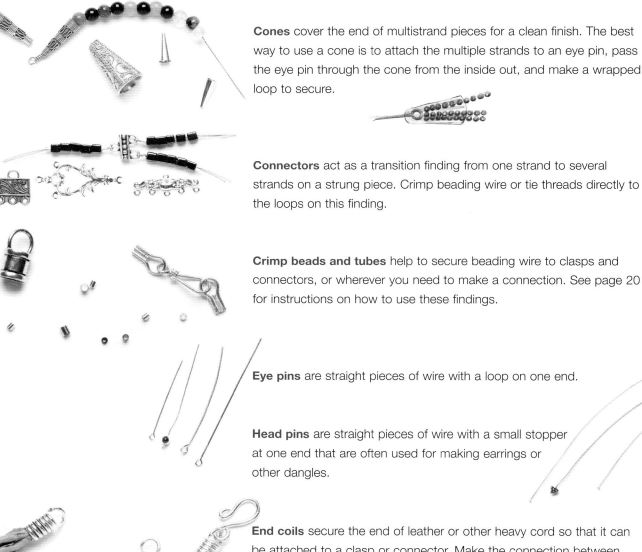

Cones cover the end of multistrand pieces for a clean finish. The best way to use a cone is to attach the multiple strands to an eye pin, pass the eye pin through the cone from the inside out, and make a wrapped loop to secure.

Connectors act as a transition finding from one strand to several strands on a strung piece. Crimp beading wire or tie threads directly to the loops on this finding.

Crimp beads and tubes help to secure beading wire to clasps and connectors, or wherever you need to make a connection. See page 20 for instructions on how to use these findings.

Eye pins are straight pieces of wire with a loop on one end.

Head pins are straight pieces of wire with a small stopper at one end that are often used for making earrings or other dangles.

End coils secure the end of leather or other heavy cord so that it can be attached to a clasp or connector. Make the connection between cord and finding by passing the cord through the coil and gently squeezing the coil with flat-nose pliers until the cord is secure.

Jump rings are small circles of wire used to connect pieces of beadwork. To open, don't bend the ends away from each other, but laterally.

Knot cups and tips help connect lightweight threads and cords to a clasp or connector. See page 26 for instructions on using knot cups. Use bead tips for the same purpose, but the knotted thread will remain exposed.

Separator bars keep multistranded jewelry bead strings separated and tidy. Use them by passing a thread or wire through a hole on the bar, string beads, and pass through the respective hole on the next bar.

Split rings are shaped like tiny key rings. They are really doubled-up jump rings that create a secure attachment because they don't open easily. You can use a split ring pliers to open split rings.

FINDINGS CHARM BRACELET

Now put all you've learned about findings into one wild bracelet. Making it will give you a lot of practice with nine types of findings, and you'll be a findings pro by the time you're finished. Because of the jangly, dangly nature of the bracelet, you've got plenty of wiggle room for mistakes. Whether you make it in silver or gold, I'm sure you'll get as many compliments as I do when I wear mine.

Materials

25 potato 7mm gold pearls

15 round butter-colored 6mm beads

12 faceted gold 5mm rondelles

Sterling silver 6mm chain

1 sterling silver 7mm split ring

30 sterling silver 6mm bead caps

7 sterling silver fish hook clasps

6 sterling silver lever back earring findings

5 sterling silver five-hole connectors

7 sterling silver knot cups

15 sterling silver head pins

8 lobster clasps

25 crimp tubes

.010 beading wire

Notions

Wire cutters

Round-nose pliers

Chain-nose pliers

Step 1: Cut the chain to your wrist size, keeping in mind the length of the lobster clasp and split ring you'll be adding as a closure. Set aside.

Step 2: Use crimp tubes and beading wire to attach the pearls to the connectors. Begin by stringing a crimp tube and a pearl. Pass through one of the loops on a connector, back through the pearl, and through the crimp tube. Snug the beads and crimp the tube. Trim the wire close to the crimp tube (Figure 1). Repeat this step for all the loops on the connector. Repeat this step for all connectors. Set aside.

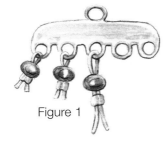

Figure 1

Step 3: String 1 bead cap, 1 round bead, and 1 bead cap on a head pin. Snug to the bottom of the pin and make a wrapped loop. Repeat this step for all bead caps and round beads.

Step 4: Slide 2 rondelles on each of the lever-back earring findings.

Step 5: Close the knot cups and loop the closure so it has no gaps.

Step 6: Attach jump rings to all the findings, bead caps, round bead dangles, and pearl-filled connectors. Spacing all evenly along the chain, attach with pliers.

3 A Bunch of Beads

Now that you've gone shopping and purchased a bunch of beads that make a nice combination, what can you do with them? Read through this chapter for some basic bead combinations.

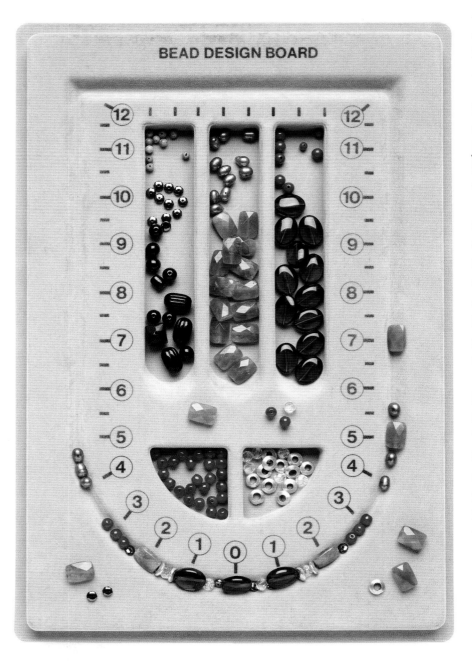

BEAD DESIGN BOARD

Think about how you will use this piece of jewelry. Will you wear it on the weekend, to work, or to the opera?

Remove the beads from their strands. The string that holds strands together is el cheapo and you don't have any use for it; throw it away! Liberate your beads! You're going to want to play with them anyway.

Buy yourself a flocked bead board with built-in grooves. This wonderful tool helps you line up beads in a pattern for a bracelet or necklace that you can easily adjust without having the beads roll onto the floor.

MAKING SOME DESIGNS

There are, of course, millions of ways to combine beads. The following pages show several examples of how you might combine the beads we show on this page. These design standbys are success stories every time.

ONE, TWO, ONE, TWO

This pattern is nice for elegant jewelry that says, "I'm pretty!" If you're making a necklace, use the pattern for a choker- or princess-length piece (see page 64). For a bracelet, you may want to stick to a single strand to keep a delicate look. This pattern is a winner for bridesmaid wear.

How to: Make two distinct bead sequence patterns and alternate them.

ONE, ONE, ONE

Repeating the same pattern throughout a piece is great for matinee-length necklaces (see page 64). With this design, you're all business. In fact, you could wear a necklace or bracelet made this way to a board meeting and garner plenty of compliments.

How to: Create one bead sequence and repeat it over and over.

PENDANT

Sometimes a necklace is more stunning with the addition of a focal piece. When you work with a pendant-style necklace stick to princess, matinee, or opera lengths (see page 64) so the pendant sits well on your chest; be sure the pendant complements, rather than detracts from, the beads.

How to: First be sure the pendant has something to make it hang straight. To do so, use a bail or make one (I used a head pin and a wrapped loop for the pendant pictured). String the pendant first and work the beads (in any pattern on these pages) out from either side. One of the most effective ways to string a necklace with a pendant is to mirror the beads on each side of the pendant.

PRETTIES ALL IN A ROW

It's okay to play favorites when it comes to beads—use this design to show them off. The resulting piece is boldly elegant, and it's best used with a matinee-length necklace (see page 64).

How to: Line up an uneven number of favorites so they sit right up front on the strand. Frame these beads with a segment of beads that contrast with the favorites, and fill out the rest of the piece with a string of smaller beads.

RANDOM

Shake up convention by throwing a bunch of beads in the air and stringing them as you pick them up. This random-design technique relies on chance, and it's great for opera-length or lariat necklaces (see page 64) and single-strand bracelets. Jewelry made this way announces that you're an *artist*.

How to: Mix up beads. Without thinking about pattern pick up the beads randomly and string them one by one until you reach the desired length.

4 Your Focal Bead

On a visit to the bead store, you may have fallen in love with a large (sometimes expensive) centerpiece bead we beaders call a focal bead. Well, now that you've got it, don't put in a drawer forever: Use it! Here are the ways I've used one focal bead in five different designs. Pick one of these general design ideas for your specific bead, or be inspired to make your own design. Come on, now, get those creative juices flowing!

MAKING PENDANTS

There are several different ways to string a focal bead. You can string it with the rest of a strand, or prepare it for use as a pendant. To create a pendant, use head pins to string the focal bead and add extra beads if you wish. If the bead is too long for a head pin, make your own pin by fashioning wire into a spiral. Finish the pendant off with a wrapped or double simple loop. (See pages 28–29 for wirework instruction.)

FIVE STRINGING IDEAS FOR FOCAL BEADS

SIMPLY RED

This necklace showcases a focal bead. Make it with simple leather cord, knots, and two beads. This minimalist style looks great with casual clothing, and the necklace can be worn short or long by sliding the knots up and down. To get the same simple look for your focal bead, choose a second smaller bead with a different shape, but in a color that complements the large bead.

Materials

1 India glass 25 x 20 bead
1 red hollow Venetian glass 50 x 25 bead
Two 1 yd (91.5 cm) lengths of round
  2mm black leather cord
One 6" (15 cm) length of round
  2mm black leather cord

Tools

Scissors

Step 1: Match the cords and tie a double-connection knot (see page 22) 3" (7.5 cm) from the ends. Tie an overhand knot on these ends.

Step 2: String the hollow bead and the India glass bead on both cords so the double-connection knot holds them.

Step 3: Tie a double-connection knot to secure the beads (Figure 1).

Step 4: Tie slide knots (see page 25) on each cord end (Figure 2) and pull very tight. Trim the extra cord close to the knot.

Step 5: Use the small length of cord to tie a slide knot on both cords (Figure 3) to keep them from separating. Tighten the knot and trim the extra cord.

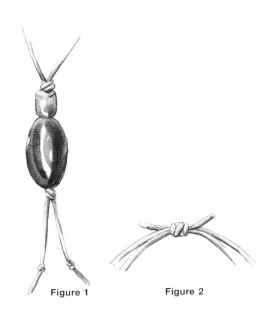

Figure 1   Figure 2

Figure 3

BIG RED

This simple necklace frames the focal bead with spots of color taken from the larger bead. You can work this matinee-length necklace up so quickly that you might want to make a matching bracelet using more bone and round beads.

M a t e r i a l s

1 red hollow Venetian glass 50 x 25 bead
6 white bone 1½" (3.81 cm) hairpipe beads
18 black 7.5mm round beads
12 red 6mm round beads
Sterling silver toggle clasp
2 sterling silver crimp tubes
Beading wire

T o o l s

Wire cutters
Crimping pliers

Step 1: Use a crimp tube to attach 21" (53.3 cm) of wire (see page 20) to one half of the clasp.

Step 2: String 1 red and 1 black bead three times.

Step 3: String 1 hairpipe, 1 black, 1 red, and 1 black bead three times.

Step 4: String the focal bead.

Step 5: String 1 black, 1 red, 1 black, and 1 hairpipe bead three times.

Step 6: String 1 black and 1 red bead three times.

Step 7: Snug the beads, string a crimp tube and attach to the other side of the clasp. Trim all tail ends close to the beads.

CRIMSON SONATA

Enhance the elegance of this opera-length necklace by adding an equally bold, but slightly smaller, bead to a second strand. This piece is suitable for the opera, of course, but would also look stunning at work.

Materials

1 red hollow Venetian glass 50 x 25 bead

1 red hollow Venetian glass 35 x 35 bead

60 black 11 x 8 Czech pressed-glass beads

24 red and gold 9 x 7 Czech pressed-glass rondelles

4 sterling silver crimp beads

Bali silver double-strand box clasp

Beading wire

Tools

Wire cutters

Crimping pliers

Step 1: Use a crimp tube to attach a 22" (56 cm) length of wire (see page 20) to the inside loop on one half of the clasp.

Step 2: String 9 black beads. String 1 rondelle and 1 black bead five times until you have 5 rondelles in all.

Step 3: String the large round bead.

Step 4: String 1 black bead and 1 rondelle five times until you have 5 rondelles in all. String 9 round beads and 1 crimp tube. Snug the beads and crimp to the inside loop on the other half of the clasp.

Step 5: String 9 black beads. String 1 rondelle and 1 black bead seven times until you have 7 rondelles in all.

Step 6: String the large oval bead.

Step 7: String 1 black bead and 1 rondelle seven times until you have 7 rondelles in all. String 9 round beads and 1 crimp tube. Snug the beads and crimp to the outside loop on the other half of the clasp. Trim all tail ends close to the beads.

HEARTBEAT SAMBA

This lariat can be created quite easily with any large focal bead. Simply choose a color (or colors) from your focal bead and make an assortment of beads in that color. Make sure you have plenty of beads to make the lariat long enough. Once you've made your necklace, try wearing it in several different ways, including wrapping it, knotting it, and looping it.

Materials

1 red hollow Venetian glass 50 x 25 bead
Assortment of black 10–12mm beads
3 silver 4mm round beads
2 silver crimp tubes
3 silver 3" head pins
Beading wire

Tools

Big eye needle
Crimping pliers
Wire cutters

Step 1: Use a head pin to string 1 silver round, 3 black beads, and 1 silver round. Make a wrapped loop (see page 29). Repeat for the other two head pins. Set aside.

Step 2: Measure the desired length of the lariat. Add 3" (7.5 cm) and cut the beading wire to that length.

Step 3: Use a crimp tube to attach the wire to one of the dangles created in Step 1 (see page 20). String 1 small black bead, the hollow bead, and enough black beads to make the desired length of the lariat.

Step 4: String a crimp tube and the two remaining dangles. Pass back through the crimp tube and a few beads on the strand. Snug all the beads and crimp the tube. Trim the wire tails.

VERMILLION BUCKS

This time the focal bead is balanced by large
Chinese lampworked beads. Their bold designs
and shape allow the focal bead to be part of the
entire design without overpowering it. When you plan
this bold type of necklace for a specific focal bead, the
design will be even more successful with spacer beads that
pick up a color in the focal bead. The spacers will visually
carry the effect of the focal bead into the rest of the piece.

Materials

1 red hollow Venetian glass 50 x 25 bead
20 multicolored 14mm Chinese lampworked beads
22 red 10mm two-faceted round beads
1 sterling silver one-to-two connector
1 sterling silver toggle clasp
6 sterling silver crimp tubes
2 silver knot cups
Beading wire

Tools

Wire cutters
Crimping pliers
Chain-nose pliers
Metal file

Step 1: Use a crimp tube to attach 12" (30.5 cm) of wire (see page 20) to one half of the clasp.

Step 2: String 1 red bead. String 1 lampworked bead and 1 red bead nine times so you have 9 lampworked beads in all.

Step 3: Snug the beads, string a crimp tube, and crimp to one loop on the double-looped side of the one-to-two connector.

Step 4: Repeat Steps 2 and 3 for the other side of the clasp (Figure 1). Set aside. Trim all tail ends close to the beads.

Figure 1

Step 5: Use 6" (15 cm) of wire to string 1 crimp tube, 1 knot cup (from inside out), 1 red bead, 1 lampworked bead, the focal bead, 1 lampworked bead, 1 red bead, 1 knot cup (from outside in), and a crimp tube. Snug the beads and crimp the tubes on the one wire. Do so without passing back through the crimp tube (Figure 2). Trim the wire close to the crimp tubes.

Figure 2

Step 6: Close the knot cups over the crimp tubes. Trim the hook off of one knot cup. File if necessary. Hook the remaining knot cup on the single side of the one-to-two connector (Figure 3).

Figure 3

5 Earrings!

Earrings are easy to make—and a great project for first-time stringers. **Most earrings involve stringing a wire with beads, making a loop, and attaching it to an earring finding. See? I told you they're easy. Here's how to make four of the most common and fashionable pairs.**

DROPS

This traditionally pear-shaped style can be made for any type of earring finding. They consist of a dangle that usually carries its weight at the bottom with smaller beads up top. But who needs to be usual? Once you've had some practice, do you own thing!

Step 1: Make a dangle by stringing an assortment of beads on a head pin (Figure 1). Be sure to leave enough room for a simple loop (⅛"/2.5 cm) or wrapped loop (1½"/3.81 cm) (see pages 28–29).

Step 2: Snug the beads and make the loop. Trim the wire end (Figure 2).

Step 3: Use a pliers to open the loop on the earring finding and attach the dangle. Close the loop. If your earring finding does not have an open loop, use a jump ring to attach the dangle to the closed loop.

Figure 1

Figure 2

HOOPS

Hoops are made for pierced ears and come in a wide range of sizes. They consist of a thin wire on which you string beads. For extra security, use a little Hypo Cement (jeweler's glue) on the wire where the beads hang. That way the beads won't slip off.

Step 1: String a few beads on the wire (Figure 1).

Step 2: If necessary, use a chain-nose pliers to slightly bend the non-loop end of the wire. This way, the wire end can lock into the loop. Let the beads slide along the wire or glue them to the wire with a small amount of Hypo Cement (Figure 2).

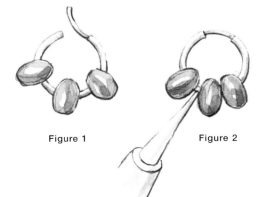

Figure 1   Figure 2

LINE

Also called stilettos because of their linear shape, these earrings can transfer easily from day wear to evening finery. Make yours on a simple head pin or experiment by using chain and attaching beads with jump rings.

Step 1: Make a dangle (see page 58) by using a head pin to string several of the same kind of beads (Figure 1). Be sure to leave enough room for a simple loop (⅛"/2.5 cm) or wrapped loop (1½"/3.81 cm).

Figure 1

Step 2: Snug the beads and make the loop. Trim the wire end (Figure 2).

Step 3: Use a pliers to open the loop on the earring finding and attach the dangle. Close the loop. If your earring finding does not have an open loop, use a jump ring to attach it to the closed loop.

Figure 2

CHANDELIER

An elegant reminder of the 1920s and 1930s, this style has become a staple in jewelry boxes. Use matte beads on dangles for daytime, crystals and chain for special occasions.

Step 1: Make as many head pin dangles (see page 58) as there are connectors. If you are using chain, make the dangles short. If you are attaching the dangles directly to a connector, make them as long as you wish (Figure 1).

Step 2: Use jump rings to attach either the dangles or short lengths of chain to the connector (Figure 2).

Step 3: If you have used chain, attach the short dangles to the bottom of the chain with jump rings (Figure 3).

Step 4: Use a round-nose pliers to open the loop on the earring finding and attach the chandelier. Close the loop. If your earring finding does not have an open loop, use a jump ring to attach it to the closed loop.

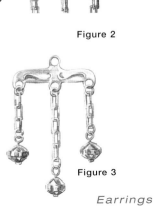

Figure 1

Figure 2

Figure 3

6 Some Design Ideas

CLASSIC JEWELRY DESIGNS

Are you ready to design your own pieces? Before you do, follow these lessons on classic jewelry design. These standards will serve as a base for what you create. Plug in your own taste, attitude, and sense of style to make my patterns your own.

CLASSIC JEWELRY LENGTHS

BRACELETS

Memory wire bracelets are made with a special, strong wire that doesn't lose its shape. The resulting bracelet fits snugly on the wrist. Bracelet memory wire is 2" (5 cm) across. Memory wire also comes in necklace and ring sizes.

Multistrand bracelets are created with the use of a multistrand clasp and are 7–8" (18–20.5 cm) in length.

Simple bracelets are composed of a single strand of beads and are 7–8" (18–20.5 cm) in length.

Stretch bracelets are created with stretch cord that fits over the hand and around the wrist.

NECKLACES

Bibs are multistrand necklaces that fit below the neckline like a bib. The top strand is shorter than the next strand, and so on.

Chokers are necklaces that fit right at the neckline and are 15–16" (38–40.5 cm) in length.

Dog collars are necklaces that fit snugly around the neck.

Lariats are claspless, unconnected beaded ropes that can be knotted, wrapped, or worn in other ways around the neck. They are usually 48" (1.3 m) in length.

Matinee necklaces fall mid-chest bone and are 20–24" (51–61 cm) in length.

Opera necklaces fall at the bottom of the chest bone and are 24–36" (61–91.5 cm) in length.

Princess necklaces fall just below the collarbone and are 18" (45.5 cm) in length.

Rope necklaces are claspless necklaces that fit over the head. They are usually 48" (1.2 m) or longer and are often knotted, flapper style.

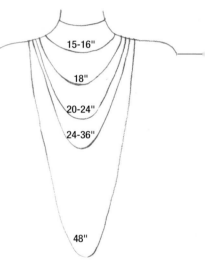

15-16"

18"

20-24"

24-36"

48"

SPARKLING STRETCH BRACELETS

These bracelets look especially attractive worn in bunches. Use fire-polished beads or crystals; sequins make an even more intriguing look.

Materials

3mm–5mm fire-polished beads
Silver crimp tubes
Clear elastic

Tools

Crimping pliers
Scissors

Step 1: String beads on elastic that has been cut to fit snugly around your wrist.

Step 2: String a crimp tube and pass the other end of the elastic back through the tube. Crimp.

REALLY SIMPLE BRACELET

This type of bracelet can look as casual or as fancy as your beads dictate. I wear mine all the time!

Materials

7–8 carnelian 12 x 8 faceted oval beads
8–9 hematite chiclet beads
14–16 Bali silver bead caps
2 silver crimp tubes
Sterling silver lobster clasp
Soldered or split ring
Beading wire

Tools

Crimping pliers
Wire cutter

Step 1: Use a crimp tube to attach 9" (23 cm) of wire to the clasp.

Step 2: String 1 chiclet, 1 bead cap, 1 oval, and 1 bead cap. Repeat this stringing sequence until the strand fits your wrist. End with 1 chiclet.

Step 3: String a crimp tube and the soldered or split ring. Pass back through the tube, snug all the beads, and crimp.

Step 4: Trim all tail wires.

PRETTY IN PINK MEMORY-WIRE BRACELET

Memory wire resembles a Slinky but doesn't lose its shape. For this particular bracelet, I've used a special type of stopper finding designed specifically for memory wire. You can also stop the beads by simply bending the wire back on itself with chain-nose pliers.

Materials

80 rhodochrosite 7 x 5 rondelles
160 Bali silver 4mm daisy spacers
78 Swarovski crystal 4mm bicone beads
2 silver memory wire stoppers
Memory wire
Hypo Cement

Tools

Heavy-duty wire cutter

Step 1: Cut a piece of memory wire with heavy-duty wire cutters, or bend the wire back and forth until it breaks. *Note:* Don't use your regular wire cutters to cut this wire or you'll mar the blades. Cut the wire so it's five coils long.

Step 2: Glue a stopper on one end of the memory wire and let dry.

Step 3: String 1 spacer, 1 rondelle, 1 spacer, and 1 crystal. Repeat until you've used all the beads, leaving about ¼" (6 mm) of the wire at the end.

Step 4: Glue a stopper on the remaining wire end and let dry.

BAROQUE MULTISTRAND BRACELET

This bold but elegant bracelet uses marcasite and fire-polished beads to evoke old-world charm. This bracelet is 7¾" (19.5 cm) long.

Materials

36 ruby 10mm fire-polished teardrop beads
18 ruby 8mm faceted rondelles
5 marcasite 25 x 5 three-hole separator bars
6 silver crimp tubes
Sterling silver 25 x 5 three-loop box clasp
Beading wire

Tools

Crimping pliers
Wire cutter

Step 1: Use a crimp tube to attach 9" (23 cm) of wire to each loop on one side of the clasp.

Step 2: Use the right wire to string 1 teardrop (point first), 1 rondelle, and 1 teardrop (bottom first). String 1 separator bar through its right hole.

Step 3: Use the middle wire to string 1 teardrop (point first), 1 rondelle, and 1 teardrop (bottom first). Pass through the separator bar strung in Step 1 through its middle hole.

Step 4: Use the left wire to string 1 teardrop (point first), 1 rondelle, and 1 teardrop (bottom first). Pass through the left hole of the separator bar strung in Step 1.

Step 5: Repeat Steps 2–4 until you've strung all the separator bars.

Step 6: String 1 teardrop (point first), 1 rondelle, and 1 teardrop (bottom first) on each wire.

Step 7: Use crimp tubes to attach each wire to its respective loop on the other side of the clasp. Trim all tail wires close to the beads.

BALI HIGH MULTISTRAND BRACELET

This bracelet uses Bali silver, known for its granulated and blackened/polished surfaces. At 7½" (19 cm) long, it looks great with casual outfits.

M a t e r i a l s

42 blue 6mm round fire-polished beads
6 Bali silver 11 x 6 two-hole separator bars
Bali silver 15 x 11 box clasp
4 silver crimp tubes
Beading wire

T o o l s

Crimping pliers
Wire cutter

Step 1: Use a crimp tube to attach 9" (23 cm) of wire to each loop on one side of the clasp.

Step 2: Use the right wire to string 3 blue beads and 1 separator bar through its right hole.

Step 3: Use the left wire to string 3 blue beads. Pass through the left hole of the separator bar strung in Step 1.

Step 4: Repeat Steps 2 and 3 until you have strung all the separator bars.

Step 5: String 3 blue beads on each wire.

Step 6: Use crimp tubes to attach each wire to its respective loop on the other side of the clasp. Trim all tail wires close to the beads.

GOLD LEAFY MULTISTRAND BRACELET

Two-holed glass beads can also be used as separator bars. Here they're a lovely olivine with gold veins. This project makes an 8" (20.5 cm) bracelet.

Materials

54 gold 5mm round fire-polished beads
7 olivine 12 x 12 leaf-shaped two-hole beads
18mm two-loop toggle clasp
4 silver crimp tubes
Beading wire

Tools

Crimping pliers
Wire cutter

Step 1: Use a crimp tube to attach 9" (23 cm) of wire to each loop on one side of the clasp.

Step 2: Use the right wire to string 3 gold beads and 1 leaf bead through its right hole.

Step 3: Use the left wire to string 3 gold beads. Pass through the left hole of the leaf bead strung in Step 1.

Step 4: Repeat Steps 2 and 3 using 4 gold beads between leaf beads until you have strung all the leaf beads.

Step 5: String 3 gold beads on each wire.

Step 6: Use crimp tubes to attach each wire to its respective loop on the other side of the clasp. Trim all tail wires close to the beads.

DISHY DOG COLLAR

This type of necklace should be worn tightly around the neck like, well, a dog collar! It has a very elegant look if you use the proper beads. In this version I've used flat beads for maximum comfort.

Materials

15–18 aventurine 10 x 15 faceted rectangular beads
16–19 sterling silver 5.5mm round beads
17mm sterling silver round box clasp
2 silver crimp tubes
Beading wire

Tools

Wire cutter
Crimping pliers
Measuring tape

Step 1: Measure around the middle of your neck. Add 3" (7.5 cm) and cut a length of wire at that measurement.

Step 2: Use a crimp tube to attach the beading wire to one side of the clasp.

Step 3: String 1 round and 1 aventurine. Repeat until the piece fits around your neck. End with 1 round.

Step 4: Use a crimp tube to attach to the other side of the clasp. Trim all wire ends.

DICHROIC CHOKER

This necklace should fit neatly around the base of your neck. These instructions are for my skinny neck, so if you need more beads to fit around your neck, add them in Step 3. If you can't find the exact supplies for this choker, just stick to the bead sizes and you'll attain the same look.

Materials

60–70 green 8mm button pearls
10–12 sterling silver 4mm round beads
12mm round dichroic pendant
8mm round dichroic box clasp
2 silver crimp tubes
Beading wire

Tools

Wire cutter
Crimping pliers

Step 1: Cut a length of wire 19" (48.5 cm) long.

Step 2: Use a crimp tube to attach the beading wire to one side of the clasp.

Step 3: String 1 round and 5 pearls. Repeat five more times.

Step 4: String the pendant.

Step 5: Repeat Step 3 in reverse order.

Step 6: String a crimp tube to attach the wire to the other side of the clasp. Trim all wire ends.

PERFECT PRINCESS NECKLACE

I've used recycled glass and silver saucers for this necklace. The simple design translates well for a variety of bead combinations.

Materials

32–34 blue 15mm faceted recycled glass beads
34–36 sterling silver 10mm saucer beads
2 sterling silver 3mm round beads
Sterling silver toggle clasp
2 silver crimp beads
Beading wire

Tools

Wire cutter
Crimping pliers

Step 1: Cut a length of wire 21" (53.5) long.

Step 2: Use a crimp tube to attach the beading wire to one side of the clasp. String 1 round bead.

Step 3: String 1 saucer and 1 blue bead. Repeat until the necklace fits just below your collarbone.

Step 4: String 1 saucer and 1 round.

Step 5: String a crimp tube to attach to the other side of the clasp. Trim all wire ends.

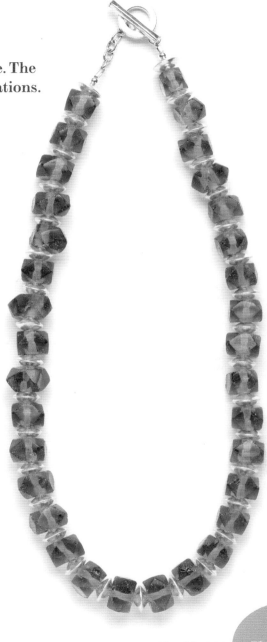

MODERN MATINEE NECKLACE

Put this necklace together with one matinee-length strand and one princess-length strand. It's a good lesson in making both a multistrand necklace and a pendant. If you have problems finding the exact materials, use the bead sizes as a shopping guide.

Materials

1 sapphire 20" (51 cm) graduated strand
   (3mm–8mm) of faceted round crystal beads
9 sapphire 9mm faceted round crystal beads
12 light blue 18mm faceted resin cube beads
9 laborodite 25 x 18 oval beads
72 sterling silver 2mm round beads or size
   11° silver seed beads
4 sterling silver 3mm round beads
4 sterling silver 4mm rondelle beads
4 silver crimp tubes
Sterling silver head pin
Sterling silver double-stranded toggle clasp
Beading wire

Tools

Wire cutter
Crimping pliers

Step 1: Make the pendant. Use the head pin to string one 3mm, 1 rondelle, 1 laborodite, 1 rondelle, and one 3mm. Snug the beads and work a wrapped loop to secure them. Set aside.

Step 2: Cut a length of wire 21" (53. 5 cm) long. Use a crimp tube to attach the wire to one loop on one side of the clasp. String 1 round and 1 rondelle. String 1 laborodite, 1 cube, one 9mm, and 1 cube three times. String one 9mm and 1 laborodite. String one 9mm for the center. Repeat this step in reverse to string the remaining wire. Use a crimp tube to attach to one loop on the other side of the clasp.

Step 3: Cut a length of wire 23" (58.5) long. Use a crimp tube to attach the wire to an open loop on one side of the clasp. Working with the graduated strand in small-est-to-largest order, string one 2mm and 1 crystal. Repeat until you come to the middle of the graduated strand. String one 2mm and the pendant you created in Step 1.

Step 4: String one 2mm and 1 crystal. Repeat, working with the gradu-ated strand from largest-to-smallest order. String one 2mm.

Step 5: Use a crimp tube to attach the wire to the remaining loop on the other side of the clasp. Trim all wire ends.

SEMIPRECIOUS OPERA NECKLACE

The length and look of this necklace makes it perfect for dressy or casual occasions. It's long enough to fit easily over the head.

M a t e r i a l s

26" (66 cm) strand of yellow jade chips
12 gold 10mm fire-polished beads
Silver or gold crimp tube
Beading wire

T o o l s

Wire cutter
Crimping pliers

Step 1: Cut a 31" (78.5 cm) length of wire.

Step 2: String 2" (5 cm) of chips and 1 gold bead twelve times.

Step 3: Use a crimp tube to secure the wire. Do so by passing the ends of the wire through the tube in opposite directions. Snug the beads and crimp the tube. Trim the wire ends.

POTATO PEARL ROPE

Wear this versatile flapper-style necklace knotted in the middle or wrapped around your neck a few times.

Materials

62" (157.5 cm) of gold potato pearls
Silver or gold crimp tube
Beading wire

Tools

Wire cutter
Crimping pliers

Step 1: Cut a 65" (165 cm) length of wire.

Step 2: String all of the pearls.

Step 3: Use a crimp tube to secure the wire. Do so by passing the ends of the wire through the tube in opposite directions. Snug the beads and crimp the tube. Trim the wire ends.

DELICATE BIB NECKLACE

This dainty necklace is made up of a mix of triangle-shaped seed, fire-polished, and round beads. Make your own mix with colors and beads that please you. Use large beads for a bold necklace.

Materials

Size 8° triangular seed beads
Assortment of 4mm fire-polished beads
Assortment of 4mm round beads
One-to-three silver connectors
S clasp
8 silver crimp tubes
Beading wire

Tools

Wire cutter
Crimping pliers

Step 1: Cut a length of wire 14" (35.5 cm) long. Use a crimp tube to attach the wire to the right loop on the three-loop side of one connector. String a random mix of beads so the strand is 11" (28 cm) long. Use a crimp tube to attach to the right loop on the other connector.

Step 2: Cut a length of wire 15" (38 cm) long. Use a crimp tube to attach the wire to the middle loop on one connector. String a random mix of beads so the strand is 12" (30.5 cm) long. Use a crimp tube to attach to the middle loop on the other connector.

Step 3: Cut a length of wire 16" (40.5 cm) long. Use a crimp tube to attach the wire to the left loop on one connector. String a random mix of beads so the strand is 13" (33 cm) long. Use a crimp tube to attach to the left loop on the other connector.

Step 4: Cut a length of wire 8" (20.5 cm) long. Use a crimp tube to attach the wire to the single loop side on the connector. String 5" (12.5 cm) of a random mix of 4mms. Use a crimp tube to attach to one side of the clasp.

Step 5: Repeat Step 4 for the other side of the clasp. Trim all wire ends.

REALLY ROSY LARIAT

This funky lariat employs multiple seed bead loops. Attach the lobster clasp at any point along the lariat so you can wear the necklace at different lengths.

Materials

Purple and pink assortment
    of India glass beads
3 purple/pink 2-hole buttons
Size 6° purple seed beads

40mm rose quartz pendant
Sterling silver lobster clasp
7 sterling silver crimp tubes
Beading wire

Tools

Wire cutter
Crimping pliers

Step 1: Leaving a 1" (2.5 cm) tail, use a 5" (12.5 cm) piece of wire to string 1 crimp tube, 1 seed bead, the clasp, and 1 seed bead. Pass down through the crimp tube and string 5 seed beads. Pass through one hole of a button. String 5 seed beads. Pass up through the crimp tube. Three wires should be running through the tube. Snug all the beads and crimp the tube. Trim the wire ends close to the beads.

Step 2: Cut a 16" (40.5 cm) length of wire. Leaving a 1" (2.5 cm) tail, string 1 crimp tube and 5 seed beads. Pass through the other hole of the button in Step 1. String 5 seed beads and pass down through the tube and crimp. Alternate stringing 1 India glass bead and 1 seed bead for 4" (10 cm). String 1 crimp tube and 5 seed beads. Pass through one hole of another button. String 5 seed beads and pass down through the tube. Snug all the beads and crimp.

Step 3: Repeat Step 2 using 9" (23 cm) of wire.

Step 4: Repeat Step 2 using 8" (20.5 cm) of wire. This time, don't finish with the button but with the rose pendant. Trim all wire ends.

ILLUSORY ROPE

When this necklace is worn, it gives the illusion of beads floating in space. The secret? A simple technique that employs multiple crimps.

Materials

10–15 gold, clear, or white 5mm or larger glass beads
20–30 gold spacer beads
20–30 gold crimp tubes
24k gold .019 beading wire
Tape

Tools

Ruler
Crimping pliers
Wire cutters

Step 1: Cut 50" of wire. String 1 crimp tube, 1 spacer, 1 bead, 1 spacer, and 1 crimp tube. Repeat this stringing sequence until you've added the desired amount of beads. Lay the wire along the edge of a work surface and tape the ends.

Step 2: Space the beads along the wire in clumps that include 1 stringing sequence from Step 1. Use a ruler to space the clumps evenly or work randomly. Leave at least 6" of bare wire at either end.

Step 3: Crimp the first tube on the first clump. Snug the beads and crimp the second crimp tube in this clump. Move down the wire to the next clump, crimping the first crimp tube, snugging the beads, and crimping the second crimp tube. Repeat until you've secured all but the last clump of beads.

Step 4: Pass the first end of the wire back through the second crimp tube of the last clump. Be sure that the spacing of this clump is in proportion to the spacing of the previous clumps. Snug the beads and crimp the tube. Trim any excess wire.

EVEN MORE DESIGN IDEAS!

When I was working with the *Beadwork* staff on stringing ideas for a special issue, I came up with these possibilities. Perhaps they'll act as springboards for your designs.

bumps on a string

pendant

one-to-three multistrand

tasseled single strand

simple focal bead with cable

long rope

donut & leather

crazy thing I saw in New York City

delicate princess

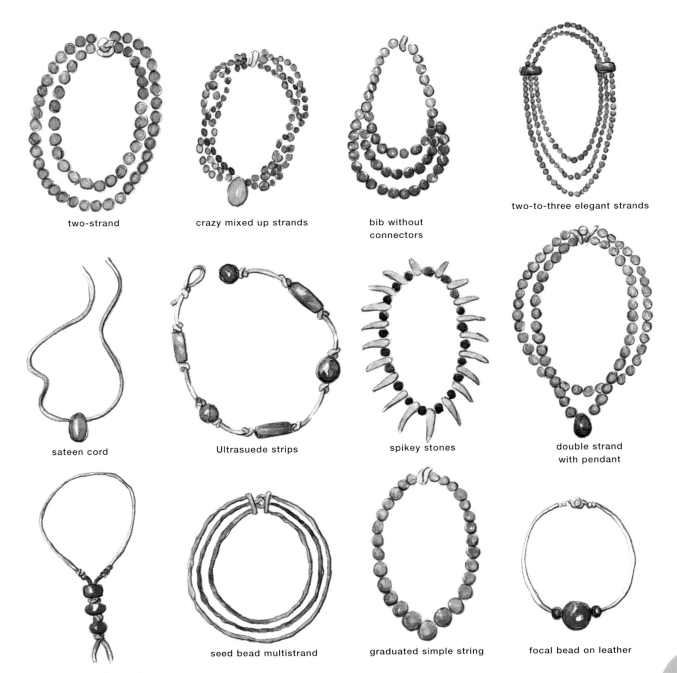

two-strand

crazy mixed up strands

bib without
connectors

two-to-three elegant strands

sateen cord

Ultrasuede strips

spikey stones

double strand
with pendant

Chinese knotted

seed bead multistrand

graduated simple string

focal bead on leather

7 Tips

- Invest in sterling silver or 24k gold findings. Not only will your work look classier, the findings will be more durable.

- Don't buy weak magnetic clasps. Strong magnetic clasps are hard to pull apart. And never use a magnetic clasp if you have a pacemaker.

- You can use continuous-hoop ear wires to make wine charms.

- Invest in good tools. They will make your beading easier and they will last longer than chintzy counterparts.

- When you buy silver, if the price seems too good to be true, it probably is.

- Keep a small measuring tape and bead-millimeter size chart with you at all times.

- Always buy more beads than you think you will need for a project.

- Invest in beautiful clasps that complement your pieces. They can often mean the difference between ho-hum and sensational work.

- When you're buying beads, be sure to ask the vendor exactly what type of bead you have bought. You'll be surprised how useful this information can turn out to be, especially when someone asks you about what you're wearing.

- Use a piece of Vellux blanket, terry cloth, velvet, or Ultrasuede as a beading surface. Your beads won't roll.

- Set up your beading surface in a low-lipped tray so that if you spill beads, you won't have to pick them up off the floor.

- Don't jeopardize your most important tool—your eyes! Make sure to bead in good light.

ON WORKING

- Don't trim tail ends until you know the crimp is satisfactory. For one reason or another, you may need to remove the crimp tube, and you can't recrimp with a short tail.

- If your beads have a nonpermanent dye or finish, try spraying the completed project with clear Krylon.

- A child's Fiskars scissors work great for cutting PowerPro and other braided threads.

- Use T-pins and a cork board, rubber bands, twist ties, or alligator clips to keep multistrand beaded cords untangled and out of the way.

- For intricate knotting techniques like macramé, the cord should be about ten times longer than the finished length of the piece.

- If you need to adjust a strung piece, and you've left enough extra wire to work with, use sharp, pointed wire cutters to cut the crimp tube free (while you carefully avoid cutting the wire). You can then rework the piece as needed and recrimp.

- Use a good jeweler's glue—Hypo Cement or E-6000—when you make jewelry; don't use "super" glues.

- Don't use crimp beads with serrated centers on nylon beading wire. The wire weakens if the nylon is pierced.

- When you're using a knot cup, first string a seed bead and bring it down to the end of the thread. Tie the thread to itself as you catch the seed bead in the knot. Next, thread the knot cup. The seed bead will act as an additional anchor.

- Keep a diamond bead reamer on hand to file out tight bead holes.

- Stand back from your work every once in a while. You can catch mistakes and admire your handiwork this way.

ON WIRE-WORKING

- Use inexpensive copper wire to practice wire techniques.

- If you use serrated pliers, cover the jaws with masking tape before you do any wirework so the pliers don't mar the wire.

- To open a jump ring, twist the ends away from each other; don't pull them apart.

- Keep a small nail file or metal file in your bead box to sand sharp wire ends.

ON MAINTENANCE

- Keep silver tarnish-free by storing it in a plastic bag that contains a piece of white chalk.

- After you shine a silver piece, rub car wax on it. Allow the wax to dry and rub it off with a soft cloth. The wax should deter tarnishing.

- You can paint a very thin layer of clear lacquer on wirework and metal beads to delay oxidation.

MATERIALS

Artgems
3850 East Baseline Rd., Ste. 119
Mesa, AZ 85206
(480) 545-6009
www.artgemsinc.com

Beadalon
(866) 423-2325
www.beadalon.com

The Bead Monkey
3717 West 50th St.
Minneapolis, MN 55410
(952) 929-4032
www.thebeadmonkey.com

Beadsmith
Helby Import Company
37 Hayward Ave.
Carteret, NJ 07008
(732) 969-5300
www.beadsmith.com
(Wholesale only)

Beyond Beadery
PO Box 460-BW
Rollinsville, CO 80474-0460
(800) 840-5548
www.beyondbeadery.com

Bobby Bead
2831 Hennepin Ave. S.
Minneapolis, MN 55408
(612) 879-8181
www.bobbybead.com

Fire Mountain Gems
One Fire Mountain Wy.
Grants Pass, OR 97526-2373
(800) 355-2137
www.firemountaingems.com

Jess Imports
66 Gough St.
San Francisco, CA 94102
(415) 626-1433
www.jessimports.com

Kamol
PO Box 95619
Seattle, WA 98145
(206) 764-7375

Klew
435 West J St.
Tehachapi, CA 93561
(661) 823-1930
www.klewexpressions.com

Knot Just Beads
515 Glenview Ave.
Milwaukee, WI 53213
(414) 771-8360

Lucky Gems
1220 Broadway, 3/F
New York, NY 10001
(212) 268-8866
www.lucky-gems.com
(Wholesale only)

Natural Touch
PO Box 351
Sonoma, CA 95476
(707) 935-7049
www.naturaltouchbeads.com

Nina Designs
PO Box 8127
Emeryville, CA 94662
(800) 336-6462
www.ninadesigns.com
(Wholesale only)

Ornamental Resources
Box 3303
1427 Miner St.
Idaho Springs, CO 80452
(800) 876-6762
Ornabead.com

Paula Radke Dichroics
www.beaduse.com

Saki Silver
362 Ludlow Ave.
Cincinnati, OH 45220
(513) 861-9626
www.sakisilver.com

Barbara Becker Simon
(239) 549-5971
www.bbsimon.com

Soft Flex Company
PO Box 80
Sonoma, CA 95476
(707) 938-3539
www.softflexcompany.com

Sweet Creek Creations
3015 Hwy. 101
Florence, OR 97439
(541) 997-0109
www.sweetcreek.com

Thunderbird Supply Company
1907 W. Historic Route 66
Gallup, NM 87301-6612
 or 2311 Vassar Northeast
Albuquerque, NM 87107-1827
(800) 545-7968
www.thunderbirdsupply.com

RESOURCES

Bateman, Sharon. *Findings and Finishings.* Loveland, Colorado: Interweave Press, 2003.

Durant, Judith, and Jean Campbell. *The Beader's Companion.* Loveland, Colorado: Interweave Press, 1998.

Griffin Bead Cord. *How to Thread a Bead Necklace.* West Germany: Griffin, n.d.

Poris, Ruth F. *Step-by-Step Bead Stringing.* 20th ed. Boynton Beach Press: Golden Hands Press, 2001.

Ward, Elizabeth. *Elizabeth Ward's Guide to Professional Bead Stringing.* Kensington, Maryland: Elizabeth Ward & Company, n.d.

INDEX